Kenneth E. Hagin

Chapter 1
HOW TO BE HEALED

That it might be fulfilled which was spoken by Esaias the prophet, saying, Himself took our INFIRMITIES, and bare our SICKNESSES.

— Matthew 8:17

Surely he hath borne our griefs [*DISEASES], *and carried our sorrows* [*PAINS].

— Isaiah 53:4

Who his own self bare our sins in his own body on the tree, that we, being dead to sins, should live unto righteousness: by whose stripes ye WERE healed.

— 1 Peter 2:24

*Literal Hebrew.

I have a twofold purpose in this lesson:

(1) To establish the scriptural fact that divine healing for our physical body belongs to us, and to help those who need healing get healed.

(2) To help those who have been healed stay healed, because it is one thing to receive something from God and another thing to maintain it.

In our first text, Matthew says he's quoting Isaiah in saying, *"Himself took our INFIRMITIES, and bare our SICKNESSES."*

Our second text says, *"Surely he hath borne our GRIEFS, and carried our SORROWS."* These translations are from the King James Version. As marginal notes in many study Bibles point out, a more accurate translation of the original Hebrew words would have been "diseases" and "pains."

After I read in my Bible that Himself took my infirmities and bare my sicknesses, I decided there wasn't any need for both Him and me to bear them, and I've been free ever since! Thank God He took our infirmities and bore our sicknesses.

One preacher said, "Well, He did it all right, but we don't have healing now in this life. We'll enjoy that blessing in the Millennium."

When I heard that fellow say it, I thought to myself, *Oh my! Either he's wrong, or God's wrong, or Jesus is wrong.*

Why? Because we won't need healing during the Millennium. We'll have a new body and we couldn't be sick anyway!

No, we need healing for the body, and we need it now—in this world. *This* world is where sickness and disease are. Blessed be God, there is healing for us in this life.

In our third text, Peter is looking back to the sacrifice of Christ when he says, "*by whose stripes ye WERE* [past tense] *healed.*"

I was reading after another supposedly outstanding Bible exponent (he must not have read the same Bible I'm reading), who said, "First Peter 2:24 doesn't mean physical healing; it refers to spiritual healing: 'By whose stripes you were healed *spiritually.*' "

Well, if he had ever read the Bible, he should know a sinner does not get healed spiritually. The human spirit of the lost man or woman is not healed—it's *reborn*. That person becomes a new creature in Christ Jesus. Old things are passed away. All things become new.

So First Peter 2:24 does not refer to spiritual healing. If you stop to think about it, friends, there is no such thing as *spiritual* healing mentioned in the Bible. The concept of *spiritual* healing came into being when some psychologists got saved and filled with the Spirit and tried to mix psychology in with the Word. They were born again, all right, and were really filled with the Holy Spirit, but they got confused.

You see, when your body gets healed, you are just healed of a disease. You've still got the same body you had before you had the disease.

If your spirit were healed, you would still have the same spirit, too, except it would just be healed. But no, blessed be God, Second Corinthians 5:17 tells us, "*Therefore if any man be in Christ, he is a NEW creature: old things are passed away; behold, all things are become NEW.*" Not half of them—all of them. Every bit of them.

In only one sense of the word could divine

healing be called spiritual healing: Our body is healed by God, and He is a Spirit. So divine healing is the Spirit's healing us, or spiritual healing. (We are not talking here about the healing of the human spirit.)

To put it another way, divine healing is not being healed spiritually, but it is spiritual because it's being healed by the power of God.

In ministering the healing power of God, I'll lay hands on people, the power of God will go into them—and often it will come right back out of them. Why?

They didn't take hold of it; usually because they are trying to receive with their mind. But *divine healing is not mental. You cannot contact God with your mind.* He is not a mind. He is a Spirit.

So healing—divine healing—God's kind of healing—is not *mental*, as Christian Science, Unity and other metaphysical teachers claim. Neither is it just *physical*, as the medical world teaches.

When God heals, He does heal you PHYSICALLY, but it is through your HUMAN SPIRIT. The reason he does is because He heals you through FAITH, and faith is of the HEART [spirit], the Bible says.

I've seen it again and again: *When people quit trying to contact God with their MINDS, and start BELIEVING in their HEARTS, they are healed instantly! "For with the HEART man BELIEVETH unto righteousness . . . ."* (Rom. 10:10).

So God contacts you through your SPIRIT—not through your MIND, and not through your BODY—because He is a Spirit. He's not a mind. He's not a man. The Bible says He isn't. Although He has a spirit-body over in the spirit world (angels do, too), God is not a PHYSICAL being. He is a Spirit. He contacts us through our spirit, and we contact Him through our spirit.

When man heals (and man can heal, whether you realize it or not), he must do it either through the mind, or through the physical senses. But when God comes on the scene as the Healer, He heals through man's spirit.

If you want to see God work, look at Jesus.

If you want to hear God talk, listen to Jesus.

Jesus told Philip, *"Have I been so long time*

with you, and yet hast thou not known me, Philip? he that hath seen me hath seen the Father" (John 14:9).

Then Jesus is God. I like to say it this way: *Jesus in His ministry is the will of God in action.*

In the ninth chapter of Mark's Gospel, for example, a man came running up to Jesus, telling Him about his demon-possessed son.

Notice what Jesus replied: *"If thou canst believe, all things are possible to him that believeth"* (v. 23). Jesus started working immediately on the man's *believing*, which had to do with his *spirit*. Jesus turned his plea for help around and said, "It's not a matter of what I can do; it's a matter of what you can believe."

"If thou canst believe, all things are possible to him that believeth."

Psalm 107:20 says, *"He sent his word, and healed them."* The Word He sent under the Old Covenant was spoken by the prophets, but the Word He sent under the New Covenant is the Lord Jesus Christ. He is the Word of God, the Living Word. He sent His Word and healed us.

Therefore, *in the mind of God, we're already healed!* He's already sent His Word and healed us! And He's given us the written Word so we'll know what the Living Word did for us.

Often God will let somebody believe for those who don't know, or those who are in the babyhood stage of Christianity. He'll meet them on a lower level of faith. But God expects mature Christians to walk in the light of what they know.

Because everybody's faith is not on the same level, God has provided seven methods by which physical healings can be obtained through the Word. (For a full explanation of these seven methods, see my book *Seven Things You Should Know About Divine Healing*.) One way is through laying on of hands.

When I lay hands on people in obedience to the Law of Contact and Transmission, the contact of my hands transmits God's healing power into their bodies to undo that which Satan has wrought, and to effect a healing and a cure in them.

When I'm conscious that the healing power went into them, I say, "There it is." That's as far as I can take people. That's where my responsibility ends and yours begins.

Chapter 2
WHAT TO DO WHEN SYMPTOMS RETURN

I've had people say to me, "Brother Hagin, when you laid hands on me, I felt the power go through me just like electricity. It went all over me. For days I was perfectly all right, but now every symptom has come back on me, and I'm worse than I ever was. Can you help me?

"Thank God, I can. Thank God, I can," I tell them. "You see, you were healed on somebody else's faith, or by a manifestation of the Spirit of God. You didn't have any foundation of the Word of God in you to help you keep your healing.

"You were like the man who built his house on the sand. The storm came and destroyed it. The symptoms came — the devil bluffed you with symptoms — you accepted them, and he put the sickness back on you."

I tell people, "The thing you must do is get to know the Lord through His Word."

As Smith Wigglesworth said, "I can't understand God by feelings. I can't understand Jesus Christ by feelings. I understand God by what the Word says about Him. He is everything the Word says He is. Get to know the Lord through the Word."

When you know that by His stripes you WERE healed—when you know that surely He has borne our diseases and carried our pains—when you know "Himself took our infirmities, and bare our sicknesses"—when you know that in your spirit as well as you know in your head that 2 + 2 = 4—then the devil will have no power over you.

When you know the power and authority of the Name of Jesus and that you have a right—a biblical right, a scriptural right—to that Name, then the devil will have no power over you.

And when symptoms come, you'll not be filled with fear. You'll simply laugh at the devil and say, "Satan, did you know you're whipped? Now you leave my body!" And he'll leave.

In August 1970, my wife and I went to Syracuse, New York, to preach a Full Gospel Business Men's Convention and to stay on for several weeks to speak for their chapters in Upper New York State.

I remember three Methodist ladies who came up to us after one of the morning services. They said, "We're new in this."

One of the ladies told me how her doctors had sent her to a hospital in New York City because they couldn't determine what was wrong with her.

After five weeks, specialists told her they had found out what was wrong, but it was incurable. She gave us the name of the disease; I had never heard of it.

"In all the history of medical science we know of only seven or eight people in the world who have ever had this," the doctors said. "There is no cure for it. We don't know exactly how long you will live; it's according to how the disease progresses. But we do know that you'll be dead within 10 years."

That's not much for a 36-year-old mother to look forward to.

She went on, "Somebody told me about wonderful healing meetings in Pittsburgh, so I went."

In the first service she attended, the Spirit of God operated in the evangelist. She pointed in this woman's direction and said, "There is a lady over here who has a very rare disease. In fact, medical science has said that only seven or eight people have ever had this."

"I was instantly healed," this woman related. "I went back to the specialists; they ran every test they could; and they couldn't find it. They said, 'We don't understand it, but it's gone.' And for months I never felt better.

"But now," she told my wife and me, "every symptom has come back on me. I haven't told my husband yet, but I'm worse than I ever was. I've been back to the meetings, but I haven't received anything. Can you help me?"

"Yes, I can," I said. "You see, you were healed by a special manifestation initiated by the Spirit of God in the life of this evangelist—and thank God for it. But then, after you got back home on your own, Satan took advantage of what you didn't know and began to put symptoms back on you. And instead of resisting them, you accepted them."

"What can I do?" she asked.

I said, "Just get in these Bible teaching services like we've been teaching here this week."

So she and her two friends began to follow us from city to city as we spoke for the various Full Gospel Business Men's chapters.

When we were getting ready to leave the area, she said, "Brother Hagin, I'm completely healed. Every symptom has disappeared. This time I got it on my own faith, and I know how to keep it. And I'll tell you something else: I know how to go out and get others healed, too."

What happened to this Methodist woman happens to many. It's easy to get healed in a mass meeting where there is a mass faith and everybody's believing. Others get healed through a special manifestation of the Holy Spirit—through gifts of the Spirit, gifts of healings, etc.

But when these people get back home on their own, they're really on their own! They're not surrounded by faith any longer. Many times they're surrounded by doubt and unbelief.

Then the minute the first symptoms show up, they say, "I *thought* the Lord healed me. I guess He didn't." And when they say that, they open the door to the devil. Instead of rising up and meeting the devil with the Word of God and commanding his power to be broken, they yield. Why? Because they have no foundation of God's Word in their lives. They are depending on others to carry them on their prayers and faith.

That might work temporarily, but a permanent healing will be based on their own faith. No one can maintain a healing which has come as a result of another's faith, gifts of the Spirit, and so on, unless his faith is developed through the Word of God to the point where he can maintain his own rights.

We must learn to say, "Devil, you can't put that back on me! The Lord has healed me. I won't accept it back." We must learn to stand in faith; to "keep the switch of faith turned on."

We know God uses people who are especially equipped and gifted by the Spirit—and thank God for them. The healing gifts bring people in. But just like new converts need to get established in the Word if they're going to go on, people who get healed need to get established in the Word if they're going to stay healed.

Years ago, when I was pastoring a Full Gospel church in the blacklands of North Central Texas, I was walking uptown to get my mail at the post office box, and I saw one of my members, Brother W______, staking his cow out in a vacant lot full of knee-deep green grass. This was 1939. (He could do that then. We didn't have all the city ordinances we have now; especially in small towns.)

As I walked up to him, he started to get up and suddenly he grabbed his back, moaning, "Ohhhh . . . . " I saw that he couldn't stand up straight, so I got hold of him and started to help him. "Oh, no, no, no! Don't touch me, Brother Hagin! Don't touch me! My goodness, that makes it worse," he said.

It took him five or ten minutes to finally stand upright. He said, "That old rheumatism has come back on me."

He was a man about 63 years old. He had been backslid for 25 years. Then I'd held a meeting in that church eight months before, and he had gotten back to God. I had laid hands on him then, and he'd been healed.

I said, "What happened, Brother W______?"

"Well," he said, "day before yesterday, I was milking the cow and the pain hit me right here in this hand, and it went up my arm and into my back. Ever since then, when I bend down, I can't get up. My back won't work right and my arm won't work right. I'm just in pain and misery."

I said, "Brother W________, you know I prayed for you last January and you were healed."

"Well, yeah," he said.

I said, "Well, how come it came back?"

"I don't know," he said.

I said, "I guarantee you that when that pain struck you in the hand and went up your arm, you said to yourself—or maybe right out loud—*I thought the Lord healed me. I guess He didn't.*"

He looked at me and said, "You must be a fortune-teller or a mind reader. That's exactly what I said!"

I said, "I'm not telling your fortune or reading your mind. I knew you had to open the door for the devil to come back in, or he couldn't have gotten back in."

He said, "That's exactly what I said."

I explained, "When you said that, you just

opened the door and said, 'Come back in, Mr. Devil, and put it on me '—and he obliged you."

"Yeah," he said, "but I'll tell you what I believe: I believe if God ever does anything, it's *done*. If God ever heals anybody, they're healed *forever*."

I said, "You mean if a fellow ever gets healed, then he's always healed?"

"Yeah."

I said, "Well, isn't that something? Jesus didn't know that. He didn't know you couldn't lose your healing or the blessings of God. When He appeared in a vision to John on the Isle of Patmos and gave him a message for one of the churches in Asia Minor, He told them to "hold fast" to what they had. Why hold fast to it if you can't lose it? There's an enemy arrayed against you who's going to do his best to rob you if he can. That's why!"

I said, "Now I'm going to ask you a question: When I laid hands on you and prayed for you last January, how long had you had this condition?"

He said, "I was in pain and I took pain medicine every day for 25 years."

I said, "Then I laid hands on your head in the Name of Jesus, every pain disappeared, and for nine months you haven't had one pain—one symptom—and you haven't taken anything for pain?"

"Not a thing," he said.

"And you said, 'I *thought* the Lord healed me.' Why, Brother W______," I said, "a 12-year-old child with half sense would know he had been healed."

He said, "Maybe I'm wrong?"

I said, "I know you're wrong."

I stood there in that vacant lot and taught him for over an hour. And he got it. He told me afterwards, "I may be a little dense, but once I get it, I've got it!" This time he got his healing and kept it.

Chapter 3
WHY FAITH IS IMPORTANT

During the great healing revival, evangelists would hold short meetings, and I'd come along behind them with longer meetings. By the time I got there, I often found people who had been healed in those meetings already had lost their healing. That happened in my meetings, too, but I learned how to get them healed and keep them healed.

In 1952, the foremost healing evangelist held a meeting in the high school auditorium in South Bend, Indiana. I was there for several meetings, and sat in a special section reserved for preachers. One of the gentlemen there was a Full Gospel pastor from Florida.

Being a minister, he could have gotten in the healing line any time he wanted to, but he was there several days, so he got a card and waited his turn. (But a minister could break in anytime; they granted them that privilege.)

This minister wore a hearing aid. He couldn't hear without it.

The night came when they called for his number. He took that hearing aid off and put it in his pocket.

Finally this preacher stepped up in place and just smiled at the evangelist. The latter said, "Well, let's see what's wrong with you." He laid hands on him and said, "Oh, oh!" He jumped back and said, "It's your ears. You're deaf." He laid hands on him, and the man's ears were opened instantly.

The evangelist had a very soft, low voice. He stood behind the man, talked in a whisper, and that fellow repeated everything he said. He was perfectly healed.

He had started to return to his seat when The evangelist said, "Hey, you're a pastor. You're a pastor of a Full Gospel church in Florida." He knew that by revelation.

Then the man came back to the preachers' section. We talked to him. He could hear everything, even when we whispered. We tested him. He was perfectly healed. But by the time the meeting was dismissed, he couldn't hear a thing. He put his hearing aid back on.

Why? He had been healed by a manifestation of the gifts of God, all right, but *if you don't have enough faith in you to hold on to what you have, the devil is going to steal it away from you.*

That's why I changed my ministry and did more teaching. Yes, I could advertise my vision, fill up an auditorium, and get many people healed—but they wouldn't keep their healing. So I held smaller meetings where I could teach the people daily in addition to ministering to the sick.

A well-known evangelist with whom I enjoy great fellowship told me the following story:

Many years ago—back in the '40s at the beginning of this brother's healing ministry—he was holding a meeting and a call came that one of the church members, a businessman with a history of heart trouble, had had a heart attack at his home.

The man's wife called the parsonage and said, "If we move him, it will kill him. But if we don't move him, he won't regain consciousness, and he'll die right here on the bedroom floor."

So the pastor and the evangelist rushed over there. They laid hands on the man and instantly he rose up well. He had been in the process of dressing, so he put on his robe and slippers, walked downstairs, and sat and talked with them for a while in the living room.

Finally the pastor and the evangelist excused themselves, and the man said, "Well, I'll go dress and go to work."

The man's wife, the evangelist said, followed them outside, closed the door, went down the front walk with them, looked around to make sure her husband couldn't hear, and said, "You all keep praying for him."

The evangelist said, "Why?"

"Why," she said, "the devil will come back and put another heart attack on him."

The evangelist said, "Sister, do you know what your problem is?"

She said, "What?"

He said, "You've got more faith in the devil than you have in God! You stood right here and told me what the devil is going to do. You believe he is going to do it. You believe he's got the authority and power to come back and put another heart attack on your husband and try to kill him. Why don't you say, 'The devil can't do it'?"

"Aw," she whispered, "I wouldn't say that for anything in the world!"

"Why?"

"Don't you know, the devil will hear me say it?"

So many Full Gospel Christians believe in the devil more than they do in God.

Have more faith in God than you do in the devil! Stand on His Word. God's Word is true. As F. F. Bosworth said, "Believe your belief and doubt your doubts."

Yes, the devil will try to put things back on you. But if the Word of God has been built into your spirit—if you've meditated on it long enough, fed on it, and put it into your spirit until you know it has become a part of your inner consciousness—you can put the devil on the run every time. If temptation comes—if pain comes—instead of being afraid and panicking, you'll just start laughing.

Chapter 4
HOW TO RESIST THE DEVIL

I was holding a meeting for a friend of mine a number of years ago when I was awakened at 1:30 in the morning by alarming symptoms in my body. (I knew something about them because I'd been born with a deformed heart and became bedfast from it. Doctors had said I could die at any minute, but I was healed by the power of God when I was 17.) These severe symptoms were in the region of my heart and chest.

The devil said to my mind, "Uh-huh, you're going to die. That's exactly what's going to happen to you. You've just been lucky you got by this far. Remember what the doctors said?"

(That sounds like him, doesn't it?)

"This is one time you're not going to get your healing," he kept repeating like a voice speaking to my mind. "Now it's all come back, and you're going to die. In fact, you're dying now."

Somebody asked me, "What did you do?"

Well, it was in the wintertime, so I pulled the covers up over my head and started laughing. Now, I didn't feel like laughing. There is such a thing as laughter inspired by the Spirit of God where you just can't help it, but I put this one on. I made myself do it. I covered my head (because I didn't want to wake up the rest of the folks in the house) and laughed out loud. It seems to me I must have laughed about 10 minutes.

Finally the devil said, "What are you laughing about?"

I said, "I'm laughing at you."

(He doesn't like to be laughed at any more than you do.) He said, "What are you laughing at me about?"

I said, "I'm laughing at you because you said I'm not going to get healed."

"That's right. That's right. This is one time you're not going to get healed."

I said, "Ha, ha, ha, ha, ha, ha, ha, ha, ha, ha, ha, ha, ha." (I just made myself do it.) I went on and on and on.

Finally the devil said for the third time,

"What are you laughing about?"

I said, "I've already told you. I'll tell you again: I'm laughing at you."

"What are you laughing at me about?"

"You said I'm not going to get healed."

"That's right. This is one time you're not going to get your healing."

I said, "Ha, ha, Mr. Devil. Sure I'm not *going* to get it. What do I need to get it for? Jesus already got it for me! I don't need to get it. All I have to do is accept it.

"Now, in case you can't read," I said, "I'll just quote First Peter 2:24 to you. It says, '*Who his own self bare our sins in his own body on the tree, that we, being dead to sins, should live unto righteousness: by whose stripes ye WERE healed.*'

"If we were, I was. So I don't have to get it; Jesus already got it for me, and because He got it for me, I accept it, claim it, and have it. Now you just gather up your little symptoms and get out of here."

You never saw anybody scurry about, gather up their belongings, and take off as fast in your life.

The Bible says to resist the devil and he'll flee from you (James 4:7). I don't know what some folks are waiting on before they start resisting. Maybe they're waiting until something comes along with long horns, a long tail, hooves, and a pitchfork.

Friends, resist anything that is of the devil and you're resisting the devil.

When doubt comes, just say, "Doubt, I resist you. I refuse to doubt."

When fear comes, speak to it. Say, "Fear, I resist you. I refuse to fear."

When sickness comes, speak to it. Say, "Sickness, I refuse to be sick. I refuse sickness. I resist you in Jesus' Name. You must go." And it will leave. You've got that right.

In a Full Gospel church in one of our western states there was a man who had been born with a deformed foot and a leg that was about four inches shorter than the other. He couldn't walk without crutches due to his crippled condition.

His deformed leg was not as big as the other one; it had not grown right. But in one of my healing meetings in the church, he got healed. His crippled leg grew out to the same length as the other, and his deformed foot straightened out. At 37 years of age, this man was able to wear the first matching pair of shoes he had ever worn in his life.

Six weeks after my meeting was over, the pastor was taking prayer requests on a Wednesday night.

A woman got up and said, "Pastor, I was healed during Brother Hagin's meeting, and for six weeks I've been all right. But all my symptoms have come back on me, and I'm worse than ever. I want you all to pray for me."

Without thinking, the pastor agreed.

Then this fellow who had been healed of the crippled foot and short leg stood up and said, "Pastor, may I say a word? I think it will help this sister.

"You all know me. I was born crippled, and I've been saved and filled with the Holy Spirit for several years now. I, too, was healed in Brother Hagin's meeting. You know I'm perfectly healed.

"Just this past week I was walking on Main Street when suddenly a pain hit me in the ankle, and that foot that had been healed turned in. I almost fell. In fact, I would have fallen if I hadn't reached my hand out and leaned against a store building. That foot turned in with such pain I could hardly stand it.

"I just slid down the wall and sat on the sidewalk. I don't know what people thought, because I picked up my ankle and foot in my hands and yelled out loud, 'No, you don't, Mr. Devil! You don't put that back on me! God's healed me.' And every symptom left. I've been all right ever since."

He maintained his healing. Although the church prayed, the women lost hers. Why? Under those conditions prayer won't work, because she already had denied what God had done.

Many times you lose by praying! You lose by turning in prayer requests! That may startle you, but what you're doing is confessing, "I don't have it."

Some years ago we were down in Greensboro, North Carolina. A woman said to me, "Brother Hagin, when you were here two years ago, I was healed of asthma and related respiratory conditions. I had been under the care of specialists for years and had spent thousands of dollars.

"For 18 solid months I never had a symptom. Then, about six months ago, every symptom of the asthma and respiratory condition came back. I almost played into the hands of the devil by accepting it, but I kept endeavoring to stand against it. I said, 'No, you can't put it back on me!' Thank God I had heard your teaching. I came every day and every night when you were here.

"My husband finally insisted that I go in for an examination. I went and the doctor said, 'I don't understand it. You've got the symptoms, but you don't have the asthma. Every test we run is negative.' "

She said, "I just spoke up and told him, 'That's that lying devil, bringing lying symptoms, trying to put it back on me!' "

"Well," the doctor said, "whatever it is, you don't have it."

She said, "I stood against it, and it disappeared. I wouldn't have known to do that if I hadn't heard your teaching." (If she had accepted it, she'd have had it back.)

I don't know why Christians don't stand against the devil and everything that is of the devil. Sickness is not of God. Sickness does not come from heaven. Sickness is not a blessing.

I'm not going to accept anything that doesn't come from heaven. I know sickness doesn't come from heaven, because there's none up there.

Someone said of their sickness, "God put it on me." Well, He stole it if He did. There's no sickness in heaven! God would have to steal it from the devil to put sickness on you. Do you see how ridiculous that is?

No, God didn't put that sickness on you—the devil did! Then he lied to you and told you God did it, and you were gullible enough to accept it.

Repeating the following confession—getting it into your spirit—will help you get and keep your healing:

Confession:

In the Name of the Lord Jesus Christ,

I exercise authority over this body of mine.

Sickness and disease, I refuse to allow you to stay.

This body, this house, belongs to God.
It is a temple of God.

Satan, you have no right to trespass on God's property.
Now you get out.
You leave my body.
I've got authority over you.
I know it,
You know it,
And God knows it.
I hold fast to what I have. I'm keeping my healing!